30 Days to Overcoming Depression & Anxiety

My Story and Personal Devotional for Fighting
Depression and Breaking Free from Anxiety

Adam Cumpston

D0071574

A special thank you to my wife, Shawna Cumpston, for
serving as my editor and giving encouragement as I lived
out this book.

Thank you to my friend Steve Breeding for your review
and input on this book.

From the Author

Are you tired of feeling like a slave to depression and anxiety?

There is hope to break the shackles that are holding you back from the life God has called you to live. I used to live a life of hopelessness and fear, but through a Biblical foundation and the power of Jesus, I have emerged as a conqueror with a renewed peace and joy.

30 Days to Overcoming Depression and Anxiety is more than just a typical Christian devotional. It details the plan that I used to transform my life and renew my mind through Christ. Each day of this journey, written from the deepest, darkest parts of my soul, tells the story of my struggle with depression, anxiety and panic attacks, and details my triumph over the things that plagued my mind.

This is more than just a fluffy, feel good book to lift your mood. Each day of this journey was written to push your limits with solid advice from the Scriptures and a daily challenge each day to bring about the needed change in your life that you desperately crave. This study is designed as a personal journey to inspire you to build a Biblical foundation in your life, giving you the tools to overcome any storm that emerges in your life.

If you are weary of the struggle to survive, you are at the right place. Let me share my story with you and show you how Jesus has totally transformed my life and made me a victor in His name. You can find victory as well!

Table of Contents

Introduction   1

Day 1 - Give Up Control   5

Day 2 - Lay Your Foundation   8

Day 3 - Build Relationships   11

Day 4 - Find Your Purpose   14

Day 5 - Confess Your Sins   17

Day 6 - Move Forward   20

Day 7 - Meditate Daily   23

Day 8 - Be Strong and Courageous   26

Day 9 - Transform Your Mind   29

Day 10 - Be Content   32

Day 11 - Give Your Treasure   34

Day 12 - Live Abundantly   36

Day 13 - Captivate Every Thought   38

Day 14 - No Condemnation   41

Day 15 - Freedom in Truth   43

Day 16 - Enjoy the Fruit   46

Day 17 - Guard Your Heart   48

Day 18 - Hope is Coming   50

Day 19 - Lifted Up   52

Day 20 - Be a Help   54

Day 21 - Cry Out to God   56

Day 22 - All Things Are Possible   58

Day 23 - God's Word is True   60

Day 24 - Wait for God   63

Day 25 - Focus Your Eyes   65

Day 26 - No Fear   68

Day 27 - Grace is Sufficient   70

Day 28 - God is Faithful   73

Day 29 - Peace Beyond Understanding   75

Day 30 - More Than a Conqueror   78

Conclusion   80

Introduction

This book holds a special place for me because it was born out of one of the most difficult and trying times of my life. After the birth of my daughter, I entered a period where anxiety consumed my life and eventually depression set in. The influences and circumstances of this world ruled my life and held me in captivity inside my mind.

Each day was miserable and seemed to be more unbearable than the last. I had completely lost my appetite and dropped over 20 pounds. I couldn't rest at night and was lucky to find 3 hours to sleep between waking up with anxiety and panic attacks. Life was no longer enjoyable. It was a drudgery that I put up with each day.

I tried everything I could do to break the shackles and end the constant barrage of negative thoughts inside my head. From internet searches to natural cures, I tried it all, but in the end, I was right back where I started.

After I figured out that I couldn't do it myself, I thought that maybe modern medicine could cure what was ailing me. I made an appointment with my doctor to get the cure-all pill that was supposed to end all of my problems. I tried an assortment of prescriptions, and with each one, the problem intensified more and more.

(FYI - I am not anti-medicine and I believe that these medicines do help a lot of people who truly need them, but I am just saying that God did not allow them to work for me this time. He had a different plan.)

After figuring out that there was nothing I could do for myself and nothing that the doctors could do, I was crushed and at the end of my rope. It felt like there was nothing really left in my power to do. At this point, the only option that I had left was to cry out to God. I finally landed at the place where I should have started in the beginning. In the middle of the day, I got on my knees and poured my heart out to Him and handed my problems over to Him.

Amazingly, things began to improve significantly that day. It still took a period of months for full recovery and rejuvenation to occur, but the change that day was instantaneous. I realized that the whole time God was simply wanting me to turn things over to Him and let Him deal with it. I wasn't made to fight the battle alone.

I wrote this 30-day devotional guide to help people who are going through similar circumstances. This is the plan that I formulated while I was battling through the raging storm. I lived this book through my recovery. The Scriptures you will read in this book can transform your life and eliminate depression, anxiety and panic attacks.

This is not your typical devotional that you will read about lifting your mood with a bunch of feel-good verses that give you temporary relief. Sure, this guide is meant to transform your mood for the better, but it addresses the root of our problems and builds us up in Christ. Until we truly begin working on the foundation and clarifying who we are in Christ, our mental state will never fully change to where we are called to be.

As you read through this guide each day, I encourage you to spend a significant amount of time, at least 10-15 minutes, meditating on the verse at the top of each day. This verse is the Word of God and it has transformational power. By incorporating it into your life and really taking time to think about it, you will see a fundamental shift in the thoughts of your mind. The words that I write below are simply thoughts to get you thinking, but always remember, they are only words written by a human. True life change will come by believing and acting on the Scriptures.

At the end of each day, there is an action that you are requested to take. The Gospel is not simply a pursuit of knowledge; rather, it is a life changing message that manifests itself through actions. Jesus didn't just call His disciples to know about Him, but He called them to take action for Him. Until you step out in faith and do what God calls you to do, you will always be wanting more and feeling like you are missing out in life.

If you haven't figured it out yet by my story, I believe that the only way to truly achieve a total transformation of your mind is through a personal relationship with Jesus Christ. He is the Rock and Foundation that my life is built on. The great news is that this relationship can be yours today. It is a free gift. It doesn't matter how much you have sinned in the past. He still loves you. All you have to do is repent and believe. Pray to Him, believe that He can forgive your sins and ask Him to do it and proclaim Jesus as Lord of your life and you will be saved.

I encourage you to reach out and contact me if you would like to learn more about a personal relationship with Jesus, share a success story of how you conquered depression or anxiety through Christ, or find out how to book me for a speaking or teaching engagement for your church or organization. You can email me at adamcumpston@gmail.com.

Enjoy the book and don't give up. Life is a battle, but when you have the King of the Universe in your corner, the victory is already yours!

Day 1

Give Up Control

"Cease striving and know that I am God;
I will be exalted among the nations, I will be exalted
in the earth."
Psalm 46:10

When I first began to struggle with anxiety and depression, I was determined to find the solution myself. I spent countless hours scouring the internet, looking for any natural way to boost my mood. I was confident that if I did my research and came up with a solid plan, I could combat this problem on my own. Well, let me tell you, I was WRONG.

Those hours of sleep and time with my family that I missed doing my "research" did not equal a cure. In fact, the independent, I-can-do-this-myself attitude, only led me to failure. I still had panic attacks. I still couldn't function in my daily life. Somewhere in the dark places of my mind, I knew I needed to try something different. So I begin the cycle of doctor visits, trips to the pharmacy, therapy appointments...all in the attempt to make my life just a little easier. NOTHING worked. In fact, when my plans failed, I spiraled even deeper into the depression that was eating me alive.

I truly believe that I went through a lot of what I did because God wanted to bring me to a place of brokenness where I realized that I was utterly helpless to change anything in my life. He let me walk through my own steps to recovery and I failed each step of the way. It wasn't until I fully let go that healing began. I couldn't conquer my issues until I realized that Jesus was the only way. Nothing I did mattered. Healing was His to give and I needed to fix my eyes on Him.

When we come to the end of our rope, that is where we find God. He tells us to quit striving and know that He is God - an ultimate form of submission to His power and authority. That seems kind of hard, doesn't it?

This is where is it is important to remember that we don't really have control of our lives anyway. Yes, God gives us the ability to think and make decisions such as what we will eat or where we will go on vacation, but when we look at the big picture, we see God at the wheel. Submission to God is not giving Him permission to take control, it is the realization and acceptance that He is already in control.

This is why the first step in recovery groups is to admit that we are powerless. Without this admission and transformation of our mindset, we will continue to spin our tires and see little or no life change because we falsely believe it is all up to us.

A full transformation of our mind requires full submission to God by entering into a healthy relationship with Jesus. Spending time in His Word daily and seeking His guidance will lead to true life change if we allow God to work in us. Your commitment to begin this 30 day journey and asking for a change of mind through Jesus is an act of submission and obedience.

Today's Challenge

Take some time today and fully survey your life. Identify areas where you are still grasping to maintain control. After you have identified these areas, turn them fully over to God. Pray for Him to assume control over these things with His mighty power and authority and ask Him to transform your mind and allow you to give up control.

Day 2

Lay Your Foundation

"Therefore everyone who hears these words of Mine and acts on them, may be compared to a wise man who built his house on the rock. And the rain fell, and the floods came, and the winds blew and slammed against that house; and yet it did not fall, for it had been founded on the rock."
Matthew 7:24,25

When building a home, laying the foundation is not really the most interesting part of the process, is it? It requires a lot of hard work and resources, and once the house it built, nobody ever sees it again. So why do people invest so much time and money to build something that nobody will ever see? This is simple. When the storms come or the ground shifts, the foundation is what holds the house together. It is the strength of the foundation that is going to keep the house from crumbling.

Prior to my struggles with depression and anxiety, my life was centered on my family, my friends and my job. My foundation in Christ was weak at best. Even though I had been saved and attended church each week, I didn't put in the hard work to build a serious relationship with Him. I was a Sunday morning warrior and assumed that would be enough to get me through life. I didn't see the storm coming and I didn't have the strong foundation needed to weather it.

You never know when a storm will hit. It can come in the form of relationship problems, financial losses, death of a loved one...really the list can go on and on. For me, it happened overnight. One day I am preparing for what should be the happiest day of my life, the birth of my daughter, and the next thing I know it is taking everything in me just to breathe. I spent the first few months of my daughter's life scrambling to put the pieces of my shattered life back together.

Let's get one thing clear, hard times are inevitable. The choice you have is how prepared you are to face them. The only foundation we can build on that will never fail us or leave us is what the Bible refers to as the Cornerstone - that is Jesus.

We build this foundation by trusting Jesus as our Savior and keeping a personal relationship with Him. This relationship is built through studying God's Word, The Bible, and spending time with Him in prayer and worship. The closer we draw to God, the stronger our foundation will be before the storms hit.

Depression and anxiety is a storm that can devastate your life. With no foundation, the battle will rage inside your mind until you feel hopeless. When your foundation is established, the storms may rage, but your hope is found in a Savior who is more powerful than any problem you may face. Don't worry if you are already in the middle of a personal storm, it is never too late to put your trust in Jesus. *(If you want to talk to me and find out more about how to get this personal relationship with Jesus, I encourage you to email me at adamcumpston@gmail.com.)*

Today's Challenge

Make a commitment today to start building your relationship with Jesus. As you read through this book each day, commit to meditating for 10-15 minutes on the featured verse at the start of each chapter and spending time in prayer with God. Be sure to keep a pencil and paper close by to write down what God is revealing to you.

Day 3

Build Relationships

And if one can overpower him who is alone, two can resist him. A cord of three strands is not quickly torn apart.
Ecclesiastes 4:12

Strength is found in numbers. This is why animals in the wild run in packs. A predator can easily pick off an individual, unassuming animal, but he has no chance of infiltrating the pack and claiming his prize. Where one is weak, many are strong.

Unfortunately, I am not a wild animal. Just a man, with too much pride and self-reliance. As the battle raged inside my mind, my natural instinct was to pull back, shut down and distance myself from those around me so they couldn't see my struggle. I had a manly image to protect and I didn't want my friends and family finding out that I was a mess.

I can still vividly remember the first time that I talked to a friend about what was going on. It wasn't because I wanted to open up, let me tell you, but my wife had told his wife and the news spread like wildfire. Since my wife had let the cat out of the bag, I was trapped in this conversation that I did not want to have. I didn't spill out my whole life story, but talking and opening up a little bit made me feel better.

Often, we are afraid to let the people we love know what is going on because we are worried what the other person will think. We isolate ourselves on our own island and feel like there is no way to escape. After that first initial conversation, I knew I had conquered a major hurdle, and I recognized that I was not meant to fight my depression and anxiety alone.

God designed us to be relational. He created us for fellowship with Him and He intends for us to fellowship with each other. This theme carries through the Bible from when God fellowshipped with Adam and Eve in the Garden of Eden to when Jesus chose His 12 disciples and spent a significant portion of His last three years mentoring and building a relationship with them.

A single piece of rope can be easily broken when tension is put on it. When rope is braided and more strands are added, the strength of the rope increases proportionally to the number of strands in the braid. The same is true for our lives. As an individual, we are weak. When tension or stress comes in our lives, we will break under the pressure if we are alone. Our resistance to breaking increases with each additional authentic relationship we are able to add.

Opportunities are around us every day to strengthen and add relationships to our lives. It is up to you to reach out and embrace them. Push past the fear and anxiety of truly opening up your life to somebody else and strive for a deep, meaningful relationship. You will be stronger for it.

Today's Challenge

Reach out today to one person and begin to build a relationship and open up with them about your life. This could mean strengthening your relationship with your spouse or spending time with somebody from church that you don't know very well. Grab a cup of coffee, go golfing, spend the day shopping, it doesn't matter what you are doing, what matters is that you are sharing your life with somebody else and building your strength.

Day 4

Find Your Purpose

*But you are A CHOSEN RACE, A royal
PRIESTHOOD, A HOLY NATION, A PEOPLE FOR
God's OWN POSSESSION, so that you may proclaim
the excellencies of Him who has called you out of
darkness into His marvelous light;*
1 Peter 2:9

You were created for a purpose. I know that may be hard to believe right now, but I can assure you that you were not placed here by accident. I have been there. I have felt the overwhelming feeling of worthlessness, that there was no point in my existence in this life. I trudged through my daily life wondering why I should try, at my job, at my relationship with my wife, at anything.

When we are feeling low and depressed, it is easy to lose our sense of purpose. Everything in our lives can start to feel meaningless. We just go through the motions of the day, not really feeling, not really accomplishing anything. We get trapped inside our minds, in our little world, in a place where we lose hope.

I am here to tell you that the purpose of your life is not simply to survive day to day. It is not to live a life of mediocrity while putting in your 70 years on this planet. God has bigger plans for you! He has designed you with special qualities and skills to accomplish the purpose He has for you. You are uniquely created, like nobody else on the face of this earth, and it is so important not to lose sight of the purpose that we have been called to in Christ.

Even though I couldn't see it at the time, I can look back now and see God's purpose for my life in all of this. When we choose to follow Christ, we come to know that we are actually chosen by God. He knows you by name. He is your biggest fan. He can encourage you and comfort you. He LOVES you when you cannot love yourself.

The God of the universe chose you to be part of His Holy Nation. How awesome is that!

The fact that God has chosen you means that He has clear plans for your life. His plans for your life probably far exceeds what you think you are capable of. His plans are not your plans. They are bigger, better, God-sized! We just need to hop on-board and let Him lead as we help to build His Kingdom.

Had I not gone through this challenging part of my life, I wouldn't be here today writing this guide for others who are struggling. My purpose never went away, it just got lost inside my mind. If this is happening to you, you need to step back and recalibrate. Just because you feel like you have no purpose doesn't mean that it is true. You just need to refresh your mind and commit to letting God show you the way to the life you were meant to live.

Today's Challenge

Spend time in prayer and meditation seeking God's purpose for your life. It may take a period of time for God to reveal your purpose, so don't give up. Once God has revealed His purpose to you, get to work. Don't delay or make excuses for what you have been called to do. Understanding and accomplishing your purpose in life will help to renew your mind.

Day 5

Confess Your Sins

Therefore, confess your sins to one another, and pray for one another so that you may be healed. The effective prayer of a righteous man can accomplish much.
James 5:16

Ok, let's face it....everybody has a past that they are not proud of. We have each done and continue to do things that make us feel ashamed and guilty. It is our sinful nature. Our human flesh.

We do our best to disguise our sins and problems by putting on a mask that the world sees. We walk around terrified that someone is going to read our minds, find out our secrets and be disgusted by our very presence. We do everything we can to look like we are happy and have everything together on the outside, but inside, we are one step away from falling over the edge.

After visiting the doctor, he suggested I visit a counselor. My first reaction was "no way." I just couldn't see what good it would do to go whine to a complete stranger about my problems. Why would he care? I didn't realize at this point the power of confession.

My first trip to the see my counselor was eye-opening. Now my thoughts were gearing more towards "why in the world didn't I do this before." It was a freeing experience. I was able to confess the things that plagued me without the fear of being judged. I could talk freely and openly for the first time. He was neutral, as many people say, he was Switzerland. Confessing my fears and my worries helped me get to the root of my problem.

When we walk around day after day with a mind full of hidden fear and worry, we get tired. All the work it takes to keep the charade of being "ok" will wear us out. Friend, without confession, it will not get better. We were not designed to keep all the garbage inside of us. We need to let it out before we are buried too deep.

There is healing in confession. Take off your mask and let another person see the real you. This small act will lift a weight off your shoulders and give you freedom. Find someone you can trust and open up about your struggles. Letting out the burdens that have held you down for years will help you to start the coping process and allow you to move on.

Sharing your heart with someone gives you a shoulder to lean on. It gives you someone who can walk the journey with you. Don't wait until your sins and problems build up to talk with them. Keep an open dialogue. Regular confession will have a freeing effect on your mind.

Today's Challenge

Find somebody you can trust to sit down with and confess any sins you may be struggling with and also confess the struggles you face inside your mind. This person could be your spouse, a family member, your friend or a pastor. If you don't have anybody you can talk to and trust, make an appointment with a counselor and open up your life to them.

Day 6

Move Forward

'For I know the plans that I have for you,' declares the LORD, 'plans for welfare and not for calamity to give you a future and a hope.
Jeremiah 29:11

One of the biggest sources of my anxiety came from my past decisions. I had made poor choices that had lasting consequences. I worried about how those choices were going to affect my present and my future. I knew I had left my past behind me and moved forward, but it still haunted me, a constant reminder of my failures. How could I trust myself to provide a good future for my family when I had made so many horrible decisions in my past?

God sees your whole life, beginning to end. Where we focus on the small things, He sees your "big picture." He knows everything about you. He knows how your life turns out. He has it all under control. Today's verse from the book of Jeremiah gives us a glimpse into God's heart for His people. His desire is not for us to go through life struggling to keep it together, living a life of despair.

He wants you to know that He is in charge. That He wants what is best for you. He wants us to have hope and a future, and the way we find this hope is through Christ.

Our past does not define us. In the Bible, the Israelites were God's chosen people. Over and over, they would make poor decisions, then cry out to God to deliver them from their consequences. As soon as God saved them from their enemies, they would turn their backs on Him once again! They never learned their lesson and they suffered tremendously. In spite of it all, God was loyal to His people and continuously came to their rescue. Even sending His only Son to die on the cross.

Just like how He was loyal to the Israelites, God is faithful to you. He knows you veer off course sometimes. He knows the path you walk isn't perfect. The only way to conquer our past is to look to Christ as your Redeemer and future. Your own strength is not enough. It is by His grace that we can let go of the past and move forward.

Today's Challenge

Write down your past sins and struggles on a piece of paper. Pray to God to forgive these sins and then burn the list in a safe area when you are done. Once the list is burned, work to forget the past and push toward the future. Remember that God is faithful to you and His plans regardless of your past problems. His grace is enough!

Day 7

Meditate Daily

But his delight is in the law of the LORD,
And in His law he meditates day and night.
He will be like a tree firmly planted by streams of
water, Which yields its fruit in its season
And its leaf does not wither;
And in whatever he does, he prospers.
Psalm 1:2-3

Meditation is a powerful tool for spiritual growth. Not the kind of meditation that is practiced by eastern religions, where you have to be overly flexible and like repeating "Ommmmmm" a hundred times, but meditation that focuses on God's Word, absorbing all it has to offer.

The Bible is FULL of much needed life insights, given by the very Creator of this world and all that is in it. This is pretty important stuff! In fact, words you read in the Bible are the MOST important words you will read in your entire life. They are the words of LIFE!

You don't want to just skim through, picking up bits and pieces. Meditation allows the Word to really speak to us. When we meditate, we can break it down into digestible pieces and really focus on how it impacts and applies to our lives. It focuses on quality over quantity. Absorbing one verse and applying it to your life trumps reading chapter after chapter with no deeper understanding.

I have read the Bible many times in my life. When I was young, my dad would have my brother and myself memorize verses. I could pull them up at a moment's notice and quote them word for word. But that didn't mean I understood them clearly. Or that I practiced what they said.

Meditation transformed my life. I was able to take a verse and truly understand its meaning and how I could apply it daily. When I get quiet and focus on God's word, I can literally feel the anxiety seep from my body with God's peace filling me back up again. I gain strength and I can readily expel the thoughts that are attacking my mind.

You must replace your own worried, anxious and depressed thoughts with the truth from the Word of God. When you begin to meditate daily, the promises of God will begin to replace the lies of the enemy inside your mind. You will become like a tree planted by the waters. Your life will flourish because what you are putting inside your mind will directly correlate to what is coming out of you.

Today's Challenge

Starting today, choose one verse each day to meditate on. Use the verse at the top of each day as you are working through this book. Spend 10 to 15 minutes meditating on the verse in the morning and think about it throughout the day. Really try to analyze each part of the verse and apply it to your life.

Day 8

Be Strong and Courageous

"Have I not commanded you? Be strong and courageous! Do not tremble or be dismayed, for the LORD your God is with you wherever you go."
Joshua 1:9

A life of timidity is no life to live.

I love international missions. It is where my heart it, it is where God leads me, it is my part of the plan God has for me. A few years ago, I joined a team going to a remote village in Honduras to install a fresh water facility and begin working on a home for a family in the community. I loved every minute of the time I spent there. When I returned, I became deathly sick. The doctors couldn't figure out what was going on. I didn't know if I was contagious, if I was going to get better or if I was going to die. My wife was 7 months pregnant with our little girl. Would I ever see her face?

This is the moment it began. Crippling fear. An unknown future. I was scared. No, I was terrified. Anxiety and depression became my daily life.

Afterwards, when I had overcame my obstacles, I had the opportunity to once again join a team going to Honduras to work in an orphanage. I readily signed up.

As the day of departure approached, my fears crept back into my mind and I started trying to find ways to get out of going. I went anyway and faced my fear. God had HUGE plans and I would have missed it if I had let my anxiety get the best of me.

God has big plans for you too.

We think we are not capable of fulfilling our calling God has given us. We miss out on life changing opportunities, memorable moments and beautiful relationships when we let our fear control us. What are we left with? A mediocre existence and a laundry list of regrets. Shew, that would make anyone depressed.

When we follow Jesus, we are called to live a life full of strength and courage. God is with us wherever we go, the Holy Spirit is our constant companion. He is there in the morning when we don't want to get out of bed. He is at our jobs when we feel inadequate or overwhelmed. He is always there, encouraging us and telling us to stay strong and finish the course.

We can't live this life on our own, but we can do all things through Christ who gives us strength (Philippians 4:13).

Today's Challenge

Identify one fear in your life that has kept you from fully reaching the purpose God has for your life. Pray for guidance from God, create a plan of how you will attack this fear and take the first step today. Remember to attack this fear with strength and courage.

Day 9

Transform Your Mind

And do not be conformed to this world, but be transformed by the renewing of your mind, so that you may prove what the will of God is, that which is good and acceptable and perfect.
Romans 12:2

When we accept Christ as our Lord, we become a new creation. Our old self passes away and we become someone new. We can't keep following our former routine. We have to start over, removing the influences of the world and replacing them with the things of God. We can't serve our sinful pleasures and Jesus at the same time.

There are different ways in which the world can overtake us. For me, it was the television. I was addicted. I could watch it for hours. I didn't screen the shows I watched. I filled my head with garbage.

When I started replacing some of the trash I watched on TV with quality alone time with God, I noticed my mind actually started to change. My thoughts started to get clearer and I began to start comprehending His great love for me. I learned that if I just stepped out of the way and quit impeding what He wanted to do, my mind would be transformed.

It is a fight every day to keep from conforming to the world. Messages we see on television and over the internet make a strong call for our minds and thoughts. The enemy is a master at marketing sin to make it look like we are missing out.

The world pollutes our minds with immoral thoughts, stress about uncertainty, and unrealistic expectations. The more we dig into God's Word, the more we will find His perfect will and force out the thoughts that will bring us down. Our mindset will shift toward Jesus.

The battle will be won by the side who gets the most input. When we are spending regular time in our Bible and diligently committed to prayer, no attack can stand against our minds and we can resist the temptations.

Keep fighting the battle and strive for the transformation of your mind. Conformity to this world is no longer an option.

Today's Challenge

Prayerfully seek out an area of your life where you are still conformed to the world. Ask God to help you end this sin and ask Him to transform your mind. Take action to eliminate this problem from your life.

Day 10

Be Content

Not that I speak from want, for I have learned to be content in whatever circumstances I am. I know how to get along with humble means, and I also know how to live in prosperity; in any and every circumstance I have learned the secret of being filled and going hungry, both of having abundance and suffering need.
Philippians 4:11-12

Be content. Hmmm, it sounds so simple doesn't it? I think we all know, that in reality, it is one of the hardest things in life to achieve. We are constantly looking at other people's lives and thinking, "If I could just have what they have..." I would be content. Happier. I would never need anything else in my entire life. Does this sound familiar?

We tend to let our circumstances define us. We focus on external factors, our job, our weight, our marriage, and we link our joy to the satisfaction we feel in those situations. Our job can be frustrating, so we are frustrated. Our weight goes up and down like a rollercoaster and our mood goes along for the ride. We base our happiness on these things instead of focusing on the only thing that can bring us true joy: Jesus.

Isn't it amazing how we can always find something to be discontent about? It is so easy! It just seems to be our natural instinct to focus on the negatives and forget about the positives in our situations. We forget about the blessings God has given us. We forget to be thankful for His love and grace.

Let's try to think about things in a different light. You may be frustrated with your job, but at least you can pay the bills. You may not like how your body looks, but at least you are healthy. You may think your marriage is lacking, but at least you have somebody to share life with.

There is always a silver lining to every problem in our lives. We just have to look over the little ant hill of our problems to see the mountain of blessings we have. It is all in our perspective. Our joy comes from seeing how life truly is with Christ, not from seeing the negatives we like to focus on.

Today's Challenge

Even though you may be discontent with several things in your life, identify the one area of dissatisfaction that causes you the most problems. Take 10 minutes and think of any positives related to this problem area. Pray and thank God for His blessings and ask Him to help you be content in this area of your life.

Day 11

Give Your Treasure

for where your treasure is, there your heart will be also.
Matthew 6:21

Did you read the verse above? I mean really read it, not just skim over it? It is one of the most simple, yet most profound verses in all of the Bible.

Now read it again, let it seep into your heart. What is your treasure? Is it your kids? Money? Drugs? Your spouse, friends, etc... Where does YOUR heart lie?

The message is so simple that I want to give it to you in the simplest way I can. I love my kids. I love my wife. But, I love Jesus more. I like having money. I like having nice things. But, I love Jesus more.

Do you see where I am going with this?

Depression and anxiety comes from putting earthly treasures before the treasures stored up for us in Heavenly places. When our priorities get out of whack, we spend countless hours worrying about things we cannot change. Our hearts ache and our souls are crushed. We become disappointed when things that we think should make us happy...don't.

If we keep working only toward our treasure in this life, we will continue to be unfulfilled. It will never be enough and we will always want more. We have to shift our mind and actions to focus on eternal treasure. This is the only way we will truly be happy with what we have.

The only treasure that will stand the test of time is that which is stored in God's Kingdom. It will never fade. The value will never go down. Thieves can't break in and steal it. Its benefits last forever.

We build this treasure by serving Christ and building the Kingdom of God. It takes us giving of ourselves to reap eternal rewards. We can give of our time and our resources. There is no small service or contribution to God when given out of a joyful and thankful heart.

Today's Challenge

Identify one area where you can serve Christ and build treasure in Heaven. It could be serving as a greeter at church, mowing your neighbor's lawn, giving money to someone in need or anything else that allows you to give of yourself with a joyful heart. Take action and complete an act of service today and continue to look for more opportunities in the future.

Day 12

Live Abundantly

"The thief comes only to steal and kill and destroy; I came that they may have life, and have it abundantly.
John 10:10

One of the saddest thoughts I have when I reflect on my journey though depression is that the enemy stole a significant period of my life. Worse, I let him do it. The time I spent laying around on the couch doing nothing was quality time I missed with my family and God. I am never going to get that time back.

The enemy is on the prowl to steal, kill and destroy our minds. He knows that if he can penetrate our thoughts and plant seeds of unhappiness or fear, we will be utterly useless to accomplish God's will. That is his game plan, but it doesn't mean he is going to win.

Jesus came so that we could have an abundant life. Struggling to make it through each day is not His goal for you. Feeling dread in the morning before you even roll out of bed is not in His plans. You are His beloved. He wants more for you. To defeat the enemy, we have to let Jesus do the work for us. We have to let Him work for our good. We serve a God who is in the life changing business. He WILL transform you, if you let Him.

I now make it a personal mission to make the most of my time. I play with my kids and have date nights with my wife. I intentionally carve out time to spend with God, reading His Word and coming to Him in prayer. You don't move forward until you make the choice to live in Jesus.

Jesus wanted that for me and He wants it for you. Choose an abundant life. Choose Jesus.

Today's Challenge

Choose an activity you have enjoyed in the past and do it today. It could be a sport, a hobby or spending time with someone you care about. Whatever it is, just do it and enjoy the life that God has given you.

Day 13

Captivate Every Thought

We are destroying speculations and every lofty thing raised up against the knowledge of God, and we are taking every thought captive to the obedience of Christ,
2 Corinthians 10:5

I don't know about you, but for me, the worst time of the day for my anxiety is bedtime. Oh man, the thoughts that can run around inside my head when the lights are off and the room is quiet. I can conjure up the most horrific thoughts, no they are not rational, but they are mine. To me, they seem so very real.

These thoughts, whether they are feasible or not, are the ammunition that fuel our anxiety. If we continuously nurture these thoughts and let them grow in our minds, we are in big trouble.

Capturing these thoughts and expelling them before they can be processed is critical. We cannot let these fantasies control our minds. When thoughts come across our mind that are contrary to God, we have to control these thoughts and banish them from our minds.

Have you ever wondered where these crazy thoughts come from? Why your mind will take one small issue and turn it into something bigger, uglier, and scarier. These thoughts are brought to you by the enemy. The prince of darkness. He wants to have you fear. He wants you to think that you are stuck with this. I am here to tell you, YOU ARE NOT!

We have the authority and ability to take every thought captive. It has been given to us by the blood of Christ Jesus.

When my thoughts are out of control, I turn to Jesus. I use the Bible as my own personal weapon. I memorize verses during the day that are relevant to my struggles and battles, and when thoughts pop into my mind at night, I just start saying these verses over and over again until my thoughts calm down and my panic attack goes away.

We must keep our minds focused on the Word of God. It is the difference in winning and losing the battle inside our mind. It is essential to being obedient to Christ. Every thought should be vetted and tested before letting it pass the precious barrier of your mind. Negative thoughts need to be checked at the door. Any thoughts that would rob you of love for God or someone else need to be thrown out quickly.

What you allow in will determine the outcome. If we strive to protect each thought, the mindset of Jesus will take over our thoughts leading us to a fuller, more joyful life.

Today's Challenge

Choose today to banish a thought from your mind that has plagued you and caused your relationship with Christ to suffer. Know that you need God's help for this. Pray to Him and ask Him to allow you to hold these thoughts captive.

Day 14

No Condemnation

*Therefore there is now no condemnation for those
who are in Christ Jesus.*
Romans 8:1

Let's talk about something that is so personal for so
many people. Something that brings us to our lowest
point. It is our feelings of inadequacy. Feeling like we
are not good enough, will never be good enough...end
of story. We will always be a failure, no matter how hard
we try or what we do. This feeling condemns us and
causes us to fall into the pit of despair.

I am here to tell you, to proclaim to you in the name of
Jesus, that you are NOT a failure, you are NOT
inadequate, you ARE good enough! The blood of Jesus
has covered your failures. If you trust in Jesus as your
Lord and Savior, condemnation is no longer a part of
your life. We have a new title - changed from
"condemned" to "redeemed." Condemnation was
crushed when Jesus rose from death in victory.

This victory is yours!

I got caught up the vicious cycle of failure and self-
condemnation. Each time I failed, I would sink lower

and it would actually drive me to fail again. This cycle easily turns into depression.

A mindset of no condemnation is one that can be difficult to accept. It clashes with everything we learn in this world. You will get pushback every day wondering if you are really forgiven. The devil will dig up the worst your past has to offer and claim that Jesus could not have possibly forgiven you for something that horrible. Don't believe him. He is the master of lies.

You are triumphant where you stand right now. Not after you change and get your life together, but just like you are in this very moment. There is nothing you can do to bring condemnation back on yourself. All of your sins, past, present and future, have been forgiven and wiped clean.

Today's Challenge

Just as Christ has forgiven us and we are no longer condemned in His eyes, we are called to do the same thing for others. Forgive somebody who has harmed you in the past. If it is possible to do so without making the situation worse, personally contact them and tell them that you have forgiven them because Christ forgave you.

Day 15

Freedom in Truth

So Jesus was saying to those Jews who had believed Him, "If you continue in My word, then you are truly disciples of Mine; and you will know the truth, and the truth will make you free."
John 8:31-32

There is freedom in truth. It may not always be convenient or pleasant to hear, but that does not alter the absolute nature of it.

When we are dealing with depression, it is easy to miss the truth and live in a lie. When I was dealing with my anxiety and depression, going into a public place, especially church, was challenging. People would ask me how I'm doing or how things were going and I always felt I had to say something positive. I lied to their faces, telling them I was fine, great, just perfect!

I wish I could tell you that I lived by what I am writing here and just told the truth about my feelings, but I didn't. I kept everything inside and continued the charade for a long time. I cringed inside every time I told another person, "I'm good." I eventually told a few select people the truth, but I wish I had the courage to tell the truth no matter who it was, no matter what my situation was.

I couldn't do it, but Jesus can. Jesus is the ultimate expression of truth. Freedom followed those who came to Him. He freed the blind and made them see. He freed the dead and gave them life. He freed the accused and forgave their sins. When people humbled themselves before Him, their lives were changed with a liberty they had never experienced before.

As followers of Christ, we are called to live a life of truth. God has given us His Word, The Bible, to reveal this truth to us. It is a direct revelation from God about how we are to live to experience a life of freedom.

Being truthful about our emotions is not very common. Unless it is someone we are close to, we give a generic "I'm ok" or "I'm fine" when we are asked about ourselves. It doesn't matter if our world feels like it is going to collapse, we still give the socially acceptable positive answer.

God did not design us to be like this. We are created to be transparent with each other, to share in our sorrows and joys with each other. You never know when you share your story with someone, you might be opening a door for them to share with you. You will find a connection that you can build on and find the support you need while helping others.

Today's Challenge

When somebody asks you today how you are doing, be honest with them. Don't tell them everything is fine when it really isn't. BE BRAVE!

Day 16

Enjoy the Fruit

But the fruit of the Spirit is love, joy, peace, patience, kindness, goodness, faithfulness, gentleness, self-control; against such things there is no law.
Galatians 5:22-23

We are halfway through our journey. Hopefully you are starting to feel God's presence in your daily life.

When we become a child of the King, we are a new creation. The old you gets taken away and replaced with a new version that strives to be more like Christ every day.

Take some time to reflect over the last 15 days. Are your thoughts becoming more like Jesus? Are your actions mimicking His? Is a transformation happening in your life right now? We do not all walk at the same pace. You may be able to answer yes. If not, your time is coming.

Just as a tree is identified by its fruit, we are identified by the attributes that we possess. So just as an apple tree produces apples and a pear tree produces pears, we produce the fruit of our spirit. If our spirit is influenced by the world, our spirit will show it.

If we follow Jesus, we have the Spirit of God living inside of us. The Holy Spirit allows us to feel joy, peace, kindness, goodness, patience, love, faithfulness, gentleness and self-control, and we can then apply them to our lives.

At this point in my journey, I was still fearful and miserable. I kept at it, building my relationship with Christ. I pushed on reading my Bible and praying. I still couldn't see the end of the tunnel, but I could feel that it was getting near.

As we grow closer to Jesus, our emotions will improve and He will lift us higher each day. His qualities will begin to work through our lives and the people around us will see a difference.

Today's Challenge

Choose one of the fruits of the Spirit and live it out today. It can be any one mentioned in Galatians, just choose one you would like to work on. Meditate on it throughout the day to see how you can implement it. Allow every action you take today to represent this fruit of the Spirit.

Day 17

Guard Your Heart

Watch over your heart with all diligence,
For from it flow the springs of life.
Proverbs 4:23

We are like a sponge when it comes to absorbing the things around us. Our attitude reflects what we allow into our heart and mind. When we drop our guard and allow thoughts into our mind that are from the world, there is no denying that they will impact our lives in a negative way.

We are bombarded every day with things that want to capture our heart. Everywhere we turn, whether it is on the television, radio, billboards or books, there is always something calling for our heart, trying to rob us of our intimacy with God.

I am a huge fan of cop dramas. As I watch these shows, the suspense builds and can cause my anxiety to flare up. Watching these bad things happen on TV can actually cause me to fear in real life. I know it sounds ridiculous, but it really happens to me. When my anxiety was at its worst, I realized that I needed to guard myself and be careful about what I put into my mind. What I was allowing to enter my mind was responsible for what was coming out of it. Think of it this way, garbage in = garbage out.

These things that compete for our heart are just another tactic of the enemy. He knows if he can drive a wedge in your heart, your relationship with Jesus will be weak and you will be susceptible to his lies over your life and mind.

We have to treat this like a battle. Surrender to the enemy is not an option. We need a plan of how we will guard our hearts, what we will stay away from. Fighting in the moment is not an effective strategy. You need to have a plan of attack before the opposing side starts to unleash their weapons. Protecting our heart and the joy it brings through a relationship with Jesus is worth the fight.

Today's Challenge

Identify and remove one area of your life that has a negative influence on your heart in Christ. This could be a particular TV show you have been watching, negative friends or the music you listen to in your car. If it is not sending a message that is consistent with the message of Christ, it is competing for your heart.

Day 18

Hope is Coming

*And not only this, but we also exult in our
tribulations, knowing that tribulation brings about
perseverance; and perseverance, proven character;
and proven character, hope;*
Romans 5:3-4

When we are right in the middle of a storm in life, we
can start to wonder what the point is. As the waves
batter us and we are gasping for air, the thought will
almost certainly cross our mind of how God could let
this happen to us. Even when we are faithful to Him,
storms still keep coming. This doesn't seem fair!

There's a big picture to all of this. We may not be able
to see it from where we stand, but God sees it all and
He has a plan. I am a different person because of the
struggles I have had with anxiety and depression. The
battle took its toll on me, but I have emerged on the
other side stronger than ever. My faith in Christ has
grown and I am a better disciple because of what I went
through.

The most explosive points of spiritual and personal
growth in our lives occur in the face of trials. This is
when our faith is tested and we really have an

opportunity to grow. Our comfortable theoretical thoughts are thrown out the window and it is sink or swim. This is when we really have a chance to depend on our Savior. Our training will emerge at this point and our foundation will shine.

Tribulation leads to perseverance, character and hope. Without facing some trials in life, our character and faith would never reach its full potential. In the middle of the storm, we will wish desperately that it would end, but after it is over and we are standing on dry ground, we will see the growth in ourselves and know that we are better for it. Keep pushing through, all storms are temporary.

Today's Challenge

Look back to a storm in your past that you have come through and think about any growth you experienced. Write this down in a journal. Keep the temporal nature of this trial and your growth in mind as you face your current trials.

Day 19

Lifted Up

I waited patiently for the LORD;
And He inclined to me and heard my cry.
He brought me up out of the pit of destruction, out of
the miry clay, And He set my feet upon a rock making
my footsteps firm.
Psalm 40:1-2

God is our great deliverer. Regardless of how bad the circumstances of our lives get, He is there as a light in the darkness. He can lift us up out of predicaments that seem impossible and hopeless. His redemption knows no bounds.

I enjoy riding ATV's. At my uncle's farm, I blaze a trail through the woods surrounding his property. Often times, I will come across a deep mud pit. Sometimes I go around, but there are other times when I can't. You have to take your chances, and occasionally you get stuck.

Life is like that. You will be going down your path and the next thing you know, you are knee deep in quick sand. Sinking deeper and deeper each day.

When we are down in the pits of life, it is important to keep calling out to God. Our emotions and fears can sometimes overwhelm us and make us feel alone, but we are never truly alone. It might be difficult to hear God's voice, but He is still there. We just need to be quiet and listen intently for that still small voice that speaks to us out of the darkness.

When God provides us deliverance, it isn't just a half-hearted pardon from our problems. No, He yanks us up out of the gutter and sticks our feet on solid ground. We can stand firm knowing that His deliverance is exactly what we need.

His timing and ours are not always the same. God grants deliverance when you need it, not when you want it. Our only option is to keep crying out to God and waiting patiently for Him. We serve a Good Father and He only wants the best for us. His deliverance will come when the time is right.

Today's Challenge

Pray today for God to deliver you from a specific area that is holding you down. Commit to pray daily for His deliverance. Be patient as you await His response and look hard to see what you can learn about Him while you are waiting.

Day 20

Be a Help

Blessed be the God and Father of our Lord Jesus Christ, the Father of mercies and God of all comfort, who comforts us in all our affliction so that we will be able to comfort those who are in any affliction with the comfort with which we ourselves are comforted by God.
2 Corinthians 1:3-4

I know that when we are facing troubles in life, it is hard to see that there is a bigger picture, a bigger purpose that we cannot see. All we can see is our suffering and heartache. It is hard to imagine that God is using us, using this experience, to further His Kingdom.

You may be wondering why God has chosen you to walk this path. I know I have wondered that a million times. As time goes on, I realize that the purpose God has for me is to reach out to others who are going through the same experiences I have. To be a light of hope in the darkness. I have been able to share my testimony with people all over the world and provide much needed encouragement. I consider my deliverance a gift that I need to share with others who need to hear that there is hope in Christ.

Going through a trial can feel like you are alone and the only person who has ever dealt with this problem. This is why God puts people in our paths, people who are struggling with the same problems that we have. We can be a shoulder for them to cry on while they are helping us work through our issues. There is mutual understanding and compassion.

If you have struggled with depression or anxiety, there is a whole world of people out there suffering and in need of your comfort. It can be difficult to open up and share your past experiences. It can even be painful to rehash old memories, but we are called to do it. Just as God comforted us, we are to comfort others.

Today's Challenge

Find somebody who is struggling with the same issues as you and talk with them. Even if you haven't completely overcome your problem yet, share with them any victories you have had and be an encouragement.

Day 21

Cry Out to God

The righteous cry, and the LORD hears
And delivers them out of all their troubles.
Psalm 34:17

I do not like asking for help. I don't really know if it is a "man thing" or just an "Adam thing," but I will avoid it at all costs. It almost cost me everything.

I was at my lowest point, the medicine the doctor gave me wasn't helping, my anxiety was at an all-time high and I really had nothing left to cling to in hopes of healing. Something deep inside me was screaming for release.

I was in my bedroom and I dropped to my knees and just poured out my heart to God. I let Him have it all. I didn't want to deal with this anymore – I couldn't deal with this anymore. I prayed for His deliverance and placed my problems at the foot of the cross.

I humbled myself before the Lord, and when I walked out of that room, I knew something was different. My situation had changed in that very instant.

Our human nature pushes us to work tirelessly to do things on our own. God wants us to cry out to Him. Our problems and feelings are not a surprise to Him. He already knows what's going on. After all, He is the God of the universe. He wants us to humble ourselves before Him and cry out to Him for help.

When your emotions sink low and depression sets in, an overwhelming feeling of helplessness can captivate your mind. It will cause you to want answers and solutions, but they will be hard to find. The solutions found in this world will sometimes just not be enough to release you from the bondage you are experiencing.

This is when it's time to cry out to God. Don't hold back anymore. When you come to Him broken and at the end of your rope, He will be there to meet you where you are and pick up the pieces for you. You have to lose your self-reliance and understand that you are helpless. It isn't a 50/50 split where you still maintain some control. When you cry out and give Him 100%, He will be there to deliver you from your troubles.

Today's Challenge

Spend some time alone today with God in prayer. Find a quiet place and lock the rest of the world out. Humble yourself before God and cry out for His help. Tell Him that you can't handle your problems anymore and ask Him to take them over and deliver you from your troubles.

Day 22

All Things Are Possible

I can do all things through Him who strengthens me.
Philippians 4:13

As believers in Christ, we are a mighty people. There is no limit to what we are capable of when we are empowered by God's Spirit in us. Everything is possible. Nothing is considered to be too great for our God to do.

If you asked me whether I would ever beat the anxiety and depression while I was in the middle of it, I would have said there is NO way. It was so strong and overpowering that it consumed my life and left me little hope for escape. I thought management of it may be feasible, but totally beating it was impossible.

In all His goodness, God has conquered the impossible and I am walking today with anxiety and depression behind me. Sure, I might have a flare up every now and then, but the issues that used to control my life are behind me and I walk a free man in the name of Jesus.

With all this power, we have to remember where it comes from. It isn't human derived or brought about by ourselves. We have no power on our own. It is only when we are connected with our Savior that we have this unbridled strength to do anything. Our power surges from the One we are connected to.

We can have victory! All hope is not lost! The strength we find in Christ is powerful enough to overcome any battle we face. Our strength is unlimited because the One who empowers us is without limit. No mountain is too great for us to overcome if Jesus is with us. No valley can get too deep if He walks through it with us.

Tackle your problems head on. Don't back down anymore. Remember that Jesus is on your side and there isn't anything that you can't do. The endless possibilities of the Creator stand with you every step of the way.

Today's Challenge

God has big plans because nothing is impossible for Him. Dream up some big plans for your life. Don't limit yourself to small stuff that is already possible for you. Dream up something big that only God could make happen and ask Him to strengthen you and make your dream a reality.

Day 23

God's Word is True

So will My word be which goes forth from My mouth;
It will not return to Me empty, Without
accomplishing what I desire, And without succeeding
in the matter for which I sent it.
Isaiah 55:11

God's Word is true. God breathed each word of the Bible into the men who would write it down. Every word was intended to accomplish His desires. Nothing was added just to take up space or to serve as a filler. It is all important. It is all relevant to our lives.

When we delve into the Word of God, we are transformed and reformed. It is a living Word and speaks the truth of God directly into our lives.

When I first started getting serious about spending time in God's Word, I had an interesting experience. I assumed that I would feel better each day as I read it, but I was wrong. For the first week or so, every time I would have my quiet time, even though I felt at peace while spending time with God, I would actually feel *more* anxious afterwards. I believe this was an attack from the devil because he saw that his grip on me was getting ready to be broken.

I considered quitting, but instead, decided that I was going to live on God's promises. When I decided to dig in my heels and serve Him because I believed in Him and knew His Word was true, the anxiety started to fade away. He delivered the peace and joy just like His Word promised that He faithfully would.

When He sends us promises through His word telling us things like we are loved regardless of our problems or that there is no reason to fear when we have His perfect love, we know that these promises are not in vain and they are guaranteed by our Creator. We simply have to believe His words are true and life changing.

It can be difficult to accept His promises when the enemy is attacking us and leading us to believe there is no hope. Our mental status wears down and the promises of God seem more like a dream than a reality. This is not the time to surrender. When the enemy is attacking, this is when we grasp onto God's Word and hold on for dear life, never letting go. His Word will prevail.

Today's Challenge

Find a promise that God has made and proclaim it over an area of your life that you have been struggling with. It could be a promise relating to guilt, fear, self-worth or anything else you struggle with. Do a quick internet search of Bible verses relating to this topic to find some verses to help you with your struggle.

Day 24

Wait for God

Wait for the LORD;
Be strong and let your heart take courage;
Yes, wait for the LORD.
Psalm 27:14

We live in a society that demands instant gratification. Our phones are glued to our fingers and we can get any information we want in a simple touch of the screen. Standard shipping takes too long so we pay extra for overnight delivery. We finance so we can get what we want NOW instead of saving our money. Waiting is not an option!

This attitude proves difficult when we are dealing with God. His timeline and ours can be totally different. He is not always in the business of providing instant fulfillment. Sometimes He likes to provide us the opportunity to wait on Him.

I can look back and see that waiting on God's timing was just what I needed. I was able to build my relationship with Him and find a deeper connection with my Savior. Waiting promotes spiritual growth, drawing us closer to Him with every second.

If God gave us our every wish like a genie in a bottle, we wouldn't need to continue to build a relationship with Him. We would just run to Him when we needed something, get our instant reward and then go back on our own path.

Waiting patiently will build character within us. It isn't easy, but it will show its rewards in the end. Waiting may seem impossible when looking to God for answers in the storms of life, but He has a purpose. In the end, good will come from your struggles if you wait patiently on Him and seek Jesus diligently.

Today's Challenge

Make a commitment today to continue waiting for God to deliver you from an area of life that you are struggling in. Keep praying daily and don't give up. Decide that you are going to live in God's time frame, not your own.

Day 25

Focus Your Eyes

And He said, "Come!" And Peter got out of the boat, and walked on the water and came toward Jesus. But seeing the wind, he became frightened, and beginning to sink, he cried out, "Lord, save me!" Immediately Jesus stretched out His hand and took hold of him, and said to him, "You of little faith, why did you doubt?"
Matthew 14:29-31

Keeping our eyes fixed on Jesus can be a struggle when there are problems swirling around us. We might have been in tune with Him before, but as worries and problems creep up on us, our mindset can shift away from Him and toward our problems. We lose focus of the One who is holding everything together.

Do you remember the story of Peter in Bible? Peter was doing just fine walking on the water until he took his eyes off Jesus and started looking at the storm. That is the moment when things fell apart and he started to sink. The wind and waves had been battering him the whole time, but they didn't present a problem until he lost his focus.

We are a lot like Peter. We may know Jesus and His power, but we still lose sight of Him when troubles descend down on us. It is so easy to claim Jesus and walk with Him when life is going smoothly and everything is falling into place, but your faith will be pushed when you have to keep focused on Him during the hard times in life.

I find that when I am stressed, feeling down or struggling with my issues, I turn to Jesus and focus my eyes on Him. But when the times are good, I drift. I start relying on myself again and what I can do. It happens time and time again. I will eventually sink back into trouble and I will refocus once again. My hope is to one day never take my eyes from the cross, but until then, I can rest in knowing Jesus is waiting for me when I return.

Even when we take our eyes off Jesus for a moment and begin to sink, there is still hope. All Peter had to do was cry out for Jesus and he was saved from the fury of the ocean. If your eyes have strayed and you have lost your sight of Christ, don't worry. Just cry out to your Savior and He will lift you up from the depths.

Today's Challenge

Regular church attendance allows us to focus our minds on Jesus as a group of worshippers each week. If you have not done so already, begin attending a church regularly and make a commitment of membership to that church.

Day 26

No Fear

There is no fear in love; but perfect love casts out fear, because fear involves punishment, and the one who fears is not perfected in love.
1 John 4:18

Fear is a part of our human nature. Without provocation, it manifests itself early in life with baseless fears such as monsters under the bed and the boogeyman. As we get older, our fears are brought on by the past experiences of ourselves or others around us. What we fear may change, but the battle with fear itself remains.

My fears raged endlessly, night after night, as I struggled to control my anxiety. I would start out thinking about the simplest, smallest thing, then, in an instant, irrational thoughts would soon invade my mind. I would spin a tale of doom and destruction, until I was sweating and shaking in fear.

When we allow fear into our minds, it can snowball out of control leaving our mental state in a total mess. One fear leads to another and that one brings a new fear with it and on and on. Fear builds on itself and eats away at our joy until only the fear remains.

It makes life unbearable. At least it did for me. I would constantly wonder what was wrong with me, knowing that these exaggerated fears were not normal. The restless nights caused me to have horrible days, where I would walk around with a tightness in my chest from all the worrying I would do.

As followers of Christ, we no longer have a reason to fear. Our fears revolve around the unknown, but with God, there is no unknown. When we serve a God who has a master plan and knows the future, we don't have to worry about what is going to happen next. We only have to trust that our Father has good plans for us and leave our fears at the foot of the cross.

It is difficult to let go of the fear that torments us. The only way to get rid of it is to replace it with love. By understanding how much God truly loves you and knowing that since He loves you, He only wants the best for you, your fears are able to be cast out and replaced by joy.

Today's Challenge

Identify the biggest fear in your life right now. Through prayer, ask God to remove this fear completely and to reveal His great love for you.

Day 27

Grace is Sufficient

And He has said to me, "My grace is sufficient for you, for power is perfected in weakness."
2 Corinthians 12:9

My daughter's middle name is Grace. We chose this name because of our struggle with infertility. Two years of treatments, hoping, praying and waiting and finally God had answered. We knew it was by His grace alone that she was to be born.

Although I saw His grace and mercy with the birth of my daughter, I didn't truly grasp the vastness of His grace until I was in the middle of my brawl with anxiety. I had so many problems, it was difficult to believe that God still loved me. I struggled to fully embrace the gift that God had given me just months before and was willing to give to me again.

The concept of grace can be difficult to fully grasp and accept. To us, it doesn't seem logical to receive rewards when our actions actually warrant punishment. We want to push back and we think there has to be a catch. God's ideas are not the same as ours. God takes His grace a step farther, by not only sparing us from the negative consequences we deserve, but actually rewarding us when we deserve to be punished.

The grace that God gives is amazing. Through Jesus, He forgives our sins when we don't deserve it and have no way to earn it. We could spend our entire lives working to attain His grace and still fall short. It isn't about whether we deserve it or if we have earned it, that is why it is grace, it is free to take if you belong to Christ. No strings attached.

His grace is sufficient. It is enough to cover all our sins and failures from the past all the way into the future. It is enough to permanently erase the guilt and shame that weighs on our minds and condemns us for our mistakes. His grace is limitless. It can't be overcome or diminished.

In order to live a life full of joy, we have to fully embrace this grace. We need to understand that we will fail, but His grace picks up the slack. It doesn't matter what we do or how badly we mess up, if we believe in Jesus, His grace is more than enough.

Today's Challenge

God has given you all the grace you will ever need. Replicate this grace toward somebody else today. When somebody does you wrong or causes you pain, give them a sincere compliment, buy them a coffee or send them a gift. Take action to show grace by illustrating that you love them even if they haven't earned it.

Day 28

God is Faithful

God is faithful, through whom you were called into
fellowship with His Son, Jesus Christ our Lord.
1 Corinthians 1:9

People always let us down. It is a sad but true reality. Whether it will be our parents, a spouse, a friend or even our children, someone will disappoint us, break our hearts and leave us to pick up the pieces. This is inevitable. The sinful nature that befell the human race in the Garden of Eden keeps us from being consistent in our faithfulness to others.

I found out the hard way I could not put my faith in my wife, my children, my job, my money or my friends to find the satisfaction and contentment I needed. Every time I put my happiness in their hands, I would be disappointed and frustrated. This would lead me even deeper into my depression. It wasn't until I put my faith in Jesus that I was able to start my healing process.

As believers in Jesus, we can count on the fact that God is faithful to us. Our actions don't determine His level of faithfulness. His love stands the test of time and overcomes all circumstances. He is walking with us through the highs and the lows. His love is consistent regardless of the situation we are in.

When we are going through hard times, it is easy to feel like God has left you and abandoned His promise to be faithful. This is when our view of God can be clouded by our own emotions. We blur the lines between what God's word says about His faithfulness and our own perceptions.

When we are able to cut through the emotions and look deeply within ourselves, we will come to the realization that God has always been there. When the storms got rough and the battle raged on, it was actually Him who kept us going and restored our strength. We can put our hope in Jesus because He is faithful.

Today's Challenge

Take some time to read about how God has been faithful in the past. Read Daniel Chapter 6 to see how God was faithful to His servant through a difficult time. This will give you encouragement as you deal with your own struggles.

Day 29

Peace Beyond Understanding

Be anxious for nothing, but in everything by prayer
and supplication with thanksgiving let your requests
be made known to God. And the peace of God, which
surpasses all comprehension, will guard your hearts
and your minds in Christ Jesus.
Philippians 4:6-7

Worrying is like sitting in a rocking chair. It gives you something to do to occupy the time, but in the end, you are at the same place you started. Worrying and anxiety have no place in the life and purpose that God has called us to. It steals our mental clarity and our valuable time, keeping us from the task at hand, furthering God's Kingdom.

God doesn't just tell us to only worry about the big things. He tells us not to worry about anything! That is a tall order to fill. It can feel like anxiety is part of our DNA. Optional and choice are not typically the words used to describe worrying. Worry almost seems natural. The only way to break the cycle is with His help. The power and direction of the Holy Spirit is required to accomplish this task.

Prayer and thanksgiving are the key components in breaking the cycle of anxiety. When you are in the middle of the storm, you may find it difficult to be thankful. You may ask the question "How can I be thankful when my world is collapsing around my feet?" Giving thanks to God might be hard but that is exactly what we are called to do. We must seek out the silver lining in our situation, no matter how big or small, and give thanks for it.

As you give thanks and spend time in prayer, something completely supernatural is going to happen to you. As the anxiety melts away, it will be replaced by a peace that transcends all understanding. Peace beyond understanding is difficult to grasp until you actually experience it. I felt like I had no hope when I was battling anxiety and depression and I really thought that I would never have peace again.

It was like a bright light turned on in my mind one day, and when my mind adjusted, I could clear my thoughts and I had a peace that I never thought I would experience. The transformation was dramatic and sudden. This change in my life was supernatural and can only be explained through divine intervention from God.

Today's Challenge

Spend a considerable amount of time in prayer today, thanking God for what He has done for you. Meditate on the things in your life that you are grateful for. You may have to dig deep, but you can start with something as little as thanking God for the air He has given you to breathe today. Take time to really analyze your life, searching out the positives that you can be thankful for. Write them down and keep them for future reference.

Day 30

More Than a Conqueror

But in all these things we overwhelmingly conquer
through Him who loved us.
Romans 8:37

Regardless of how we may feel right now, our battle has already been won! Jesus has already conquered death, hell and the grave. This is great news! A clear and decisive winner has been crowned in the cosmic battle between good and evil. We still have to fight in this life due to our fallen nature, but the final score has already been guaranteed.

As co-heirs with Christ, we share in this victory. Since He conquered, we in turn have conquered because we are found in Him. His victory is our victory. When we died to ourselves and took up our cross like Jesus, we were instantly granted the status of conqueror. Our destiny was secured at that point and nothing can change it.

I have walked through this battle and emerged because I am a conqueror in Christ. When I finally realized the battle was not mine to win alone, but rather mine to win in Him, the sea parted and the clouds rolled back allowing me to walk through triumphantly in victory. I stand on the other side of this battle now looking back with the enemy defeated in Christ. This experience has taught me that nothing in this world and no attack brought on by the enemy has any dominion or power over me. The fears that still try to come into my mind, the dissatisfaction with my current circumstances, and my worries about the future no longer chain me down and keep me a prisoner in my own mind. My strength and victory lies in the resurrected King, and just as He has already conquered this world, so have I. So can you!

Put your mind in Heavenly places and claim the promises of God. Depression, anxiety, fear or any other problem you face have absolutely no dominion over you. They have already been crushed in a triumphant victory by our Savior and Lord. The war has been fought and the victory won in the name of Jesus.

All that is left to do now is claim this victory and live each day as a conqueror in Christ.

Today's Challenge

We need to be reminded daily of the fact that we have conquered everything through Jesus. Verbally declare this over your life each morning when you get out of bed. As problems arise during the day, declare it again. Use this truth in your battles with the enemy and claim the victory that is already rightfully yours.

Conclusion

I sincerely hope that this book has been a blessing to you. I encourage you to continue spending time with God daily, building a personal relationship that will be your firm foundation in the years to come. Whether this is your first time dealing with depression and anxiety or these issues have followed you around your entire life, there is a way out. There is hope for everyone to overcome their strongholds through the blood of Jesus Christ. He wants you, and He is willing to meet you where you are.

If you can spare a few seconds, I would really appreciate it if you would leave me a review on Amazon. Thanks!

If you have any questions or have an interest in me speaking with your group, feel free to contact me by email at adamcumpston@gmail.com.

Thanks for reading! God bless!